This Book Belongs To:

First Name : ....

Last Name : ....

هذا الكتاب الخاص بـ :

الإسم الشخصي : ....

الإسم العائلي : ....

Fruits

◇━━━◇

Grape عنب	Apple تفاح
Berry توت	Peach خوخ
Cherry كرز	Fig تين
Lemon ليمون	Orange برتقال
Avocado أفوكادو	Apricot مشمش
Banana موز	Kiwi كيوي

Fruits

Pear إجاص	Mango مانجو
Nectarine دراق	Plum برقوق
Raisin زبيب	Papaya بابايا
Pomegranate رمان	Melon شمام
Watermelon بطيخ	Persimmon كاكي
Pineapple أناناس	Strawberry فراولة

Vegetables

Carrot	Celery
جزر	كرفس
Garlic	Tomato
ثوم	طماطم
Okra	Onion
بامية	بصل
Radish	Potato
فجل	بطاطس
Corn	Beetroot
ذرة	بنجر
Parsley	Cabbage
بقدونس	ملفوف

Vegetables

Pumpkin يقطين	Beans فاصولياء
Lettuce خس	Chickpeas حمص
Eggplant باذنجان	Green Peas بازلاء
Mushrooms فطر	Zucchini كوسة
Spinach سبانخ	Bell pepper فلفل حلو
Artichokes خرشوف	Chile pepper فلفل حار

Colors

Black أسود	**White** أبيض
Yellow أصفر	**Red** أحمر
Blue أزرق	**Brown** بني
Pink زهري	**Green** أخضر
Rose وردي	**Grey** رمادي
Gold ذهبي	**Orange** برتقالي

Medicine

Patient مريض	Doctor طبيب
Diseases مرض	Medicine طب
Hospital مستشفى	Operation عملية
Health صحة	Ambulance اسعاف
Anesthesia تخدير	Clinic عيادة
Pharmacy صيدلية	Dentist طبيب الاسنان

Arts

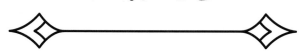

Actor ممثل	Music موسيقى
Movie فيلم	Artist فنان
Novel رواية	Star نجم
Book كتاب	Writer كاتب
Melody لحن	Song أغنية
Composer ملحن	Poetry شعر

Animals

Snail حلزون	Lion أسد
Camel جمل	Cat قطة
Frog ضفدع	Pig خنزير
Wolf ذئب	Dog كلب
Eagle نسر	Chicken دجاجة
Donkey حمار	Parrot ببغاء

Animals

Cow بقرة	Owl بومة
Snake ثعبان	Lamb خروف
Crow غراب	Bull ثور
Calf عجل	Fish سمك
Duck بطة	Goat ماعز
Horse حصان	Rabbit أرنب

City

Cafe مقهى	Church كنيسة
Bank بنك	School مدرسة
Bakery مخبز	Hotel فندق
Mosque جامع	Theater مسرح
Bar حانة	Company شركة
Street شارع	House بيت

City

Museum متحف	Airport مطار
Zoo حديقة الحيوان	Palace قصر
Library مكتبة	Shop محل
Club نادي	Road طريق
Restaurant مطعم	University جامعة
Building عمارة	Apartment شقة

Body

Eye عين	Head رأس
Nose أنف	Hand يد
Liver كبد	Lung رئة
Vein عرق	Stomach معدة
Knee ركبة	Shoulder كتف
Neck رقبة	Beard لحية

Body

Skin جلد	**Hair** شعر
Arm ذراع	**Ear** أذن
Face وجه	**Leg** رجل
Heart قلب	**Abdomen** بطن
Finger اصبع	**Tooth** سن
Tongue لسان	**Mouth** فم

Numbers

One واحد	Two إثنان
Three ثلاثة	Four أربعة
Five خمسة	Six ستة
Seven سبعة	Eight ثمانية
Nine تسعة	Ten عشرة
Hundred مائة	Million مليون

Clothing

◇————————◇

Dress فستان	**Pants** سروال
Hat قبعة	**Shoe** حذاء
Shirt قميص	**Skirt** تنورة
Sock جورب	**Jacket** سترة
Belt حزام	**Coat** معطف
Glasses نظارة	**Blouse** بلوزة

Emotions

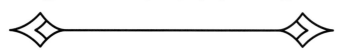

Sad حزين	Love حب
Shy خجول	Happy سعيد
Stressed متوتر	Hate كراهية
Revile سب	Depressed مكتئب
Calm هادئ	Angry غاضب
Passion عشق	Worries هموم

Work

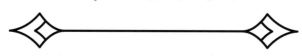

Salary مرتب	Job وظيفة
Money مال	Resume سيرة
Office مكتب	Boss مدير
Promotion ترقية	Resigned استقال
Retire تقاعد	Colleague زميل
Employment توظيف	Unemployment بطالة

Work

Doctor طبيب	Designer مصمم
Trainer مدرب	Artist فنان
Lawyer محامي	Engineer مهندس
Carpenter نجار	Barber حلاق
Agent وكيل	Contractor مقاول
Butcher جزار	Accountant محاسب

House

Door باب	Window نافذة
Kitchen مطبخ	Room غرفة
Wall حائط	Lamp مصباح
Closet خزانة	Mirror مرآة
Stairs درج	Floor أرضية
Faucet صنبور	Bathroom حمام

Kitchen

Fork شوكة	Pan مقلاة
Plate طبق	Oven فرن
Knife سكين	Glass كأس
Pot قدر	Spoon ملعقة
Stove موقد	Microwave ميكروويف
Fridge ثلاجة	Blender خلاط

Sports

Ball كرة	Player لاعب
Hockey هوكي	Golf غولف
Skiing تزلج	Boxing ملاكمة
Swimming سباحة	Chess شطرنج
Volleyball كرة الطائرة	Tennis كرة المضرب
Soccer كرة القدم	Basketball كرة السلة

Family Members

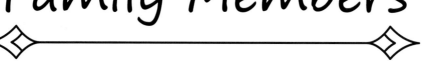

Father أب	Mother أم
Brother أخ	Sister أخت
Uncle خال - عم	Aunt خالة - عمة
Grandson حفيد	Granddaughter حفيدة
Niece ابنة الأخ - الأخت	Nephew ابن الأخ - الأخت
Grandfather جد	Grandmother جدة

Transportation

Car سيارة	Train قطار
Taxi تاكسي	Bus حافلة
Boat قارب	Brakes فرامل
Truck شاحنة	Plane طائرة
Bicycle دراجة	Ship سفينة
Police Car سيارة شرطة	Ambulance سيارة اسعاف